Someone's sitting in the shade today because someone planted a tree a long time ago.
—Warren Buffett

MY
WARREN BUFFETT
BIBLE

*A Short and Simple Guide to
Rational Investing:* 284 Quotes from the
World's Most Successful Investor

Edited by
ROBERT L. BLOCH

Program Officer of The H&R Block Foundation
Treasurer and Director of the
Marion and Henry Bloch Family Foundation

Reproduced from copywritten material with permission of owner.

Skyhorse Publishing

Skyhorse Publishing books may be purchased in bulk at special discounts for sales promotion, corporate gifts, fund-raising, or educational purposes. Special editions can also be created to specifications. For details, contact the Special Sales Department, Skyhorse Publishing, 307 West 36th Street, 11th Floor, New York, NY 10018 or info@skyhorsepublishing.com.

Skyhorse® and Skyhorse Publishing® are registered trademarks of Skyhorse Publishing, Inc. ®, a Delaware corporation.

Visit our website at www.skyhorsepublishing.com.

10 9 8 7 6 5 4 3 2

Library of Congress Cataloging-in-Publication Data is available on file.

Print ISBN: 978-1-63450-557-4
Ebook ISBN: 978-1-63450-994-7

Cover design by Anthony Morais

Printed in the United States of America

MY
WARREN BUFFETT
BIBLE

Over a decade ago, I had the good fortune to meet Warren Buffett when he became a major shareholder in H&R Block, the tax preparation company my father, Henry Bloch, co-founded in 1955.

Warren and my father have much in common. Both entrepreneurs were born before World War II in the Mid-West and came from middle class families. They are extremely down to earth and have loads of good common sense and honesty. Without a doubt, both enjoy "the process more than the proceeds" of business and investing.

Buffett's investment principles are "simple, old, and few." Much like my father, most of Warren's success is due to his personality, character, and willingness to learn from and teach others. Of his many outstanding qualities, the role as teacher is the one for which, Warren states, he would most like to be remembered.

Recently I have made Warren my teacher and mentor by reading and re-reading his quotes until they have become a part of me. As the "Oracle of Omaha" said, "It's better to hang out with people better than you. Pick out associates whose behavior is better than yours and you'll drift in that direction." As investors, we should all strive to drift toward Warren's direction.

There have been dozens of books published that have attempted to capture the philosophy and personality of Warren Buffett; but words cannot really describe this amazing man ... except maybe his own words. Buffett does Buffett better than anyone. Since Warren has never written an autobiography, the quotes in this book are the most direct and unfiltered source we have.

After experiencing several bear markets over his lifetime, Warren has learned to stay the course and stick to his investing principles, when other investors were selling or rethinking their strategies. Therefore a proven discipline is an essential element in becoming a successful investor. This book has helped me become a more disciplined investor.

I am confident it will not only help you become more disciplined but also a more RATIONAL, OPTIMISTIC, and LONG-TERM investor. The ultimate act of generosity is Warren Buffett sharing his genius with the individual investor!

—Robert L. Bloch

Note: I am honored that Warren Buffett has given me written permission to use his inspiring words in this volume.

Opportunities abound in America.

In the business world, the rearview mirror is always clearer than the windshield.

American business will do just fine over time. And stocks will do well just as certainly, since their fate is tied to business performance. Periodic setbacks will occur, yes, but investors and managers are in a game heavily stacked in their favor. (The Dow Jones Industrials advanced from 66 to 11,497 in the twentieth century, a staggering 17,320% increase that materialized despite four costly wars, a Great Depression, and many recessions. And don't forget that shareholders received substantial dividends throughout the century as well.)

Risk comes from not knowing what you are doing.

Since the basic game is so favorable, Charlie* and I believe it's a terrible mistake to try to dance in and out of it based upon the turn of tarot cards, the predictions of "experts," or the ebb and flow of business activity. The risks of being out of the game are huge compared to the risks of being in it.

---

* Charlie Munger is the vice-chairman of Berkshire Hathaway.

It is more important to say "no" to an opportunity,
than say "yes."

∞

Look at market fluctuations as your friend rather
than your enemy; profit from folly rather than participate in it.

It's better to hang out with people better than you. Pick out associates whose behavior is better than yours and you'll drift in that direction.

∽∞∾

To swim a fast 100 meters, it's better to swim with the tide than to work on your stroke.

Wall Street is the only place that people ride to in a Rolls-Royce to get advice from those who take the subway.

∝∞∝

I never attempt to make money on the stock market. I buy on the assumption that they could close the market the next day and not reopen it for five years.

Buy companies with strong histories of profitability and with a dominant business franchise.

⌐◯⌐

Rule No. 1: Never lose money.
Rule No. 2: Don't forget No. 1.

When I buy a stock, I think of it in terms of buying a whole company, just as if I were buying the store down the street. If I were buying the store, I'd want to know all about it. I mean, look at what Walt Disney was worth on the stock market in the first half of 1966. The price per share was $53, and this didn't look especially cheap; but on that basis, you could buy the whole company for $80 million when "Snow White," "Swiss Family Robinson," and some other cartoons, which had been written off the books, were worth that much; and then you had Disneyland and Walt Disney, a genius, as a partner.

You don't want a capital market that functions perfectly if you're in my business. People continue to do foolish things no matter what the regulation is, and they always will.

⚬≫⚬

We went from a wooded land to an incredible, absolute abundance of riches because the United States has had a system that can unleash human potential. Never bet against what humans can accomplish if they're operating in the right soil. And we have the right soil.

The products or services that have wide, sustainable moats around them are the ones that deliver rewards to investors.

❧

You only find out who is swimming naked when the tide goes out.

A great investment opportunity occurs when a marvelous business encounters a one-time huge, but solvable problem.

∞

We believe that a policy of portfolio concentration may well decrease risk if it raises, as it should, both the intensity with which an investor thinks about a business and the comfort level he must feel with its economic characteristics before buying into it.

I don't look to jump over 7-foot bars: I look around for 1-foot bars that I can step over.

⚮

Overall, we've done better by avoiding dragons than by slaying them.

Should you find yourself in a chronically leaking boat, energy devoted to changing vessels is likely to be more productive than energy devoted to patching leaks.

∽∞∽

It's far better to buy a wonderful company at a fair price than a fair company at a wonderful price.

People who buy [stocks] for non-value reasons are likely to sell for non-value reasons. Their presence in the picture will accentuate erratic price swings unrelated to underlying business developments.

∞

With enough insider information and a million dollars, you can go broke in a year.

If you are not going to be an active investor—and very few should try to do that—then they should just stay with index funds. Any low-cost index funds. And they should buy it over time. They're not going to be able to pick the right price and the right time. What they want to do is avoid the wrong price and the wrong stock. You just make sure you own a piece of American business, and you don't buy all at one time.

A truly great business must have an enduring "moat" that protects excellent returns on invested capital. Business history is filled with "Roman candles," companies whose moats prove illusory and were soon crossed.

❦

Startups are not our game.
(*Many of Berkshire Hathaway's largest holdings are well over a century old; American Express, Wells Fargo, Procter & Gamble, and Coca-Cola were started in 1850, 1852, 1837, and 1886, respectively.*)

You only have to do a very few things right in your life so long as you don't do too many things wrong.

∞

When we own portions of outstanding businesses with outstanding managements, our favorite holding period is forever.

Berkshire's ownership interest in all four companies [Coca-Cola, American Express, IBM, and Wells Fargo] is likely to increase in the future. Mae West had it right: "Too much of a good thing can be wonderful."

∞

The business schools reward difficult complex behavior more than simple behavior, but simple behavior is more effective.

I will tell you how to become rich. Close the doors. Be fearful when others are greedy. Be greedy when others are fearful.

∾⧓∾

If you buy things you do not need, soon you will have to sell things you need.

Like Wayne Gretzky says, go where the puck is going,
not where it is.

∞

Long ago, Ben Graham taught me that "price is what you
pay; value is what you get." Whether we're talking about
socks or stocks, I like buying quality merchandise when it is
marked down.

Before looking at new investments, we consider adding to old ones. If a business is attractive enough to buy once, it may well pay to repeat the process.

Americans are in a cycle of fear which leads to people not wanting to spend and not wanting to make investments, and that leads to more fear. We'll break out of it. It takes time.

This is the one thing I can never understand. To refer to a personal taste of mine, I'm going to buy hamburgers the rest of my life. When hamburgers go down in price, we sing "Hallelujah Chorus" in the Buffett household. When hamburgers go up, we weep. For most people, it's the same way with everything in life they will be buying—except stocks. When stocks go down and you can get more for your money, people don't like them anymore.

Only buy something you'd be perfectly happy to hold if the market shut down for 10 years.

∽

The stock market is a non-called strike game. You don't have to swing at everything—you can wait for your pitch. The problem when you're a money manager is that your fans keep yelling, "Swing you bum!"

I don't invest a dime based on macro forecasts.

When investing, pessimism is your friend, euphoria the enemy.

The American economy is going to do fine. But it won't do fine every year and every week and every month. I mean, if you don't believe that, forget about buying stocks anyway. But it stands to reason. I mean, we get more productive every year, you know. It's a positive-sum game, long term. And the only way an investor can get killed is by high fees or by trying to outsmart the market.

The ability to say "no" is a tremendous advantage
for an investor.

∞

It's been an ideal period for investors: A climate of fear is their
friend. Those who invest only when commentators are upbeat end
up paying a heavy price for meaningless reassurance.

Tax-paying investors will realize a far, far greater sum from a single investment that compounds internally at a given rate than from a succession of investments compounding at the same rate.

⸎

The investor today does not profit from yesterday's growth.

A thought for my fellow CEOs: Of course, the immediate future is uncertain, America has faced the unknown since 1776. It's just that sometimes people focus on the myriad of uncertainties that always exist while at other times they ignore them (usually because the recent past has been uneventful).

∽◊∾

If you own See's Candy, and you look in the mirror and say, "Mirror, mirror on the wall, how much do I charge for candy this fall?" and it says, "More," that's a good business.

Time is the friend of the wonderful company, the enemy of the mediocre.

If a business does well, the stock eventually follows.

In stocks, we expect every commitment to work out well because we concentrate on conservatively financed businesses with strong competitive strengths, run by able and honest people. If we buy into these companies at sensible prices, losses should be rare.

❧

Never invest in a business you can't understand.

You should invest in a business that even a fool can run,
because someday a fool will.

Much success can be attributed to inactivity. Most investors cannot resist the temptation to constantly buy and sell.

Though the path has not been smooth, our economic system has worked extraordinarily well over time. It has unleashed human potential as no other system has, and it will continue to do so. America's best days lie ahead.

There are 309 million people out there that are trying to improve their lot in life. And we've got a system that allows them to do it.

The reaction of my family and me to our extraordinary good fortune is not guilt, but rather gratitude. Were we to use more than 1% of my claim checks on ourselves, neither our happiness nor well-being would be enhanced. In contrast, that remaining 99% can have a huge effect on the health and welfare of others. That reality sets an obvious course for me and my family: Keep all we can conceivably need and distribute the rest to society, for its needs. My pledge starts us down that course.

It is optimism that is the enemy of the rational buyer.

∽◈∾

But I think it is very easy to see what is likely to happen over the long term. Ben Graham told us why: "Though the stock market functions as a voting machine in the short run, it acts as a weighing machine in the long run." Fear and greed play important roles when votes are being cast, but they don't register on the scale.

Today people who hold cash equivalents feel comfortable. They shouldn't. They have opted for a terrible long-term asset, one that pays virtually nothing and is certain to depreciate in value.

❧

Charlie Munger made me focus on the merits of a great business with tremendously growing earning power; but only when you can be sure of it—not like Texas Instruments or Polaroid, where the earning power was hypothetical.

The definition of a great company is one that will be great for 25 or 30 years.

⌒∞⌒

Success in investing doesn't correlate with IQ. Once you have ordinary intelligence, what you need is the temperament to control the urges that get other people in trouble investing.

There seems to be some perverse human characteristic that likes to make easy things difficult.

᨞

Periodically, financial markets will become divorced from reality.

Tomorrow is always uncertain. Don't let that reality spook you. Throughout my lifetime, politicians and pundits have constantly moaned about terrifying problems facing America. Yet our citizens now live an astonishing six times better than when I was born. The prophets of doom have overlooked the all-important factor that is certain: Human potential is far from exhausted, and the American system for unleashing that potential—a system that has worked wonders for over two centuries despite frequent interruptions for recessions and even a Civil War—remain alive and effective.

I tell everybody who works for our company to do only two things to be successful. They are 1) think like an owner, and 2) tell us bad news right away. There is no reason to worry about good news.

⌦

It's far better to own a portion of the Hope diamond than 100 percent of a rhinestone.

Do not take yearly results too seriously. Instead, focus on four-or five-year averages.

∽∞∾

We are not natively smarter than we were when our country was founded nor do we work harder. But look around you and see a world beyond the dreams of any colonial citizen. Now, as in 1776, 1861, 1932, and 1941, America's best days lie ahead.

Inactivity strikes us as intelligent behavior.

We will continue to ignore political and economic forecasts, which are an expensive distraction for many investors and businessmen.

What the wise do in the beginning, fools do in the end.

❧

You do things when the opportunities come along. I've had periods in my life when I've had a bundle of ideas come along, and I've had long dry spells. If I get an idea next week, I'll do something. If not, I won't do a damn thing.

There are speed handicappers and class handicappers. The
speed handicapper says you try and figure out how fast the
horse can run. A class handicapper says a $10,000 horse will
beat a $6,000 horse. [Ben] Graham says, "Buy any stock cheap
enough, and it will work." That was the speed handicapper.
And other people said, "Buy the best company, and it will
work." That's class handicapping.

In fact, the true investor welcomes volatility . . . because a wildly fluctuating market means that irrationally low prices will periodically be better attached to solid businesses. It is impossible to see how the availability of such prices can be thought of as increasing the hazards for an investor who is totally free to either ignore the market or exploit its folly.

Turnarounds seldom **turn**.

A prediction about the direction of the stock market tells you nothing about where stocks are headed, but a whole lot about the person doing the predicting.

We always live in an uncertain world. What is certain is that
the United States will go forward over time.

∽⧖∽

We have a wonderful system that eventually is self-cleansing
and always moves forward.

Five years from now, 10 years from now, the world everywhere will be doing better.

⁓∞⁓

Our system unleashes people's potential. And we've got 312 million people that want to do better tomorrow than today. Over time, that works. This country goes forward, and it'll continue to go forward. The luckiest person in history on a probability basis is the baby being born in the United States today.

I am not a businessman, I am an artist.

∞

A number of smart people are involved in running hedge funds. But to a great extent their efforts are self-neutralizing, and their IQ will not overcome the costs they impose on investors. Investors, on average and over time, will do better with a low-cost index fund than with a group of funds.

So if the government rate rises, the prices of all other investments must adjust downward, to a level that brings their expected rates of return into line. Conversely, if government interest rates fall, the move pushes the prices of all other investments upward.

∽∾

No business has ever failed with happy customers. You are selling happiness.

Most analysts feel they must choose between two approaches customarily thought to be in opposition: "value" and "growth." . . . In our opinion, the two approaches are joined at the hip: Growth is always a component in the calculation of value.

✼

We're not looking at the aspects of the stock, we're looking at the aspects of the business.

Post mortems of acquisitions, in which reality is honestly compared to the original price projections, are rare in American boardrooms. They should be standard practice.

Our stay-put behavior reflects our view that stock market serves as a relocation center at which money is moved from the active to the patient.

We have long felt that the only value of stock forecasters is to make fortune-tellers look good. Even now, Charlie [Munger] and I continue to believe that short-term market forecasts are poison and should be kept locked up in a safe place, away from children and also from grown-ups who behave in the market like children.

In stock markets it's an auction market, and crazy things can happen.

∽

When people get fearful, they get fearful en masse. Confidence comes back one at a time. When they get greedy, they get greedy en masse.

You can't make a good deal with a bad person.

We will have another bubble, but usually you don't get it the same way you got it before.

In any business, there are going to be all kinds of factors that happen next week, next month, next year, and so forth. But the really important thing is to be in the right business. The classic case is Coca-Cola, which went public in 1919. They initially sold stock at $40 a share. The next year, it went down to $19. Sugar prices had changed pretty dramatically after World War 1. So you would have lost half of your money one year later if you'd bought the stock when it first came public; but if you owned that share today—and had reinvested all of your dividends—it would be worth about $1.8 million. We have had depressions. We have had wars. Sugar prices have gone up and down. A million things have happened. How much more fruitful is it for us to think about whether the product is likely to sustain itself and its economies than to try to be questioning whether to jump in or out of the stock?

If you're in the luckiest 1% of humanity, you owe it to the rest of humanity to think about the other 99%.

⌘

There are some parts of the game that we don't understand, so we don't play with them.

[*On economic forecasts:*] Why spend time talking about something you don't know anything about? People do it all the time, but why do it?

❧

The best thing that happens to us is when a great company gets into temporary trouble…We want to buy them when they're on the operating table.

My own preference is an investment in productive assets, whether businesses, farms, or real estate. Ideally, these assets should have the ability in inflationary times to deliver output that will retain its purchasing-power value while requiring a minimum of new capital investments. Farms, real estate, and many businesses such as Coca-Cola, IBM, and our own See's Candy meet that double-barreled test.

Most advisors are far better at generating high fees than they are at generating high returns.

∽◈∾

I think the most important factor in getting out of the recession actually is just the regenerative capacity of American capitalism.

To invest successfully, you need not understand beta, efficient markets, modern portfolio theory, option pricing, or emerging markets. You may, in fact, be better off knowing nothing of these. That, of course, is not prevailing view at most business schools, whose finance curriculum tends to be dominated by such subjects. In our view, though, investment students need only two well-taught courses—How to Value a Business, and How to Think About Market Prices.

When proper temperament joins with proper intellectual framework, then you get rational behavior.

Overwhelmingly, for people that can invest over time, equities are the best place to put their money. Bonds might be the worst place to put their money. They are paying very, very little, and they're denominated in a currency that will decline in value.

If principles can become dated, they're not principles.

∞

Owning businesses is much more interesting than owning gold or farmland. Besides, stocks are probably still the best of all the poor alternatives in an era of inflation—at least they are if you buy in at appropriate prices.

If you feel that you can dance in and out of securities in a way that defeats the inflation tax, I would like to be your broker— but not your partner.

The fact that people will be full of greed, fear, or folly is predictable. The sequence is not predictable.

We enjoy the process far more than the proceeds.

∽∾

Charlie [Munger] and I never have an opinion on the market because it wouldn't be any good and it might interfere with the opinions we have that are good.

The market is there only as a reference point to see if anybody is offering to do anything foolish. When we invest in stocks, we invest in businesses.

∽

For some reason, people take their cues from price action rather than from values. What doesn't work is when you start doing things that you don't understand or because they worked last week for somebody else. The dumbest reason in the world to buy a stock is because it's going up.

If past history was all there was to the game, the richest people would be librarians.

❦

Market forecasters will fill your ear but never fill your wallet.

I only get into situations where I know the value. There are thousands of companies whose value I don't know. But I know the ones I know. And incidentally you don't pinpoint things. If somebody walks in this door and they weigh between 300 and 350 pounds, I don't need to say they weigh 327 to say that they're fat.

John Maynard Keynes essentially said, Don't try to figure out what the market is doing. Figure out a business you understand, and concentrate.

I like to go for cinches. I like to shoot fish in a barrel. But I like to do it after the water has run out.

❦

Overall, Berkshire and its long-term shareholders benefit from a sinking stock market much as a regular purchaser of food benefits from declining food prices. So when the market plummets—as it will from time to time—neither panic nor mourn. It's good news for Berkshire.

Currently liking neither stocks nor bonds, I find myself the polar opposite of Mae West as she declared, "I only like two kinds of men: foreign and domestic."

Valuing a business is part art and part science.

Berkshire buys when the lemmings are heading
the other way.

∞

Writing a check separates a commitment from a conversation.

When Charlie [Munger] and I buy stocks—which we think of as small portions of businesses—our analysis is very similar to that which we use in buying entire businesses. We have to decide whether we can sensibly estimate an earnings range for five years out, or more. If the answer is yes, we will buy the stock (or business) if it sells at a reasonable price in relation to the bottom boundary of our estimate. If, however, we lack the ability to estimate future earnings—which is usually the case— we simply move on to other prospects.

When you're associating with the people that you love, doing what you love, it doesn't get any better than that.

❧

In a bull market, one must avoid the error of the preening duck that quacks boastfully after a torrential rainstorm, thinking that its paddling skills have caused it to rise in the world. A right-thinking duck would instead compare its position after the downpour to that of the other ducks on the pond.

Most people get interested in stocks when everyone else is. The time to get interested is when no one else is. You can't buy what is popular and do well.

〰

You don't need to be a rocket scientist. Investing is not a game where the guy with the 160 IQ beats the guy with a 130 IQ. Rationality is essential.

We like stocks that generate high returns on invested capital where there is a strong likelihood that it will continue to do so. For example, the last time we bought Coca-Cola, it was selling at about 23 times earnings. Using our purchase price and today's earnings, that makes it about 5 times earnings. It's really the interaction of capital employed, the return on that capital, and future capital generated versus the purchase price today.

As long as we can make an annual 15 percent return on equity, I don't worry about one quarter's results.

The propensity to gamble is always increased by a large prize versus a small entry fee, no matter how poor the true odds may be. That's why Las Vegas casinos advertise big jackpots and why state lotteries headline big prizes.

Great investment opportunities come around when excellent companies are surrounded by unusual circumstances that cause the stock to be misappraised.

Draw a circle around the businesses you understand and then
eliminate those that fail to qualify on the basis of value, good
management, and limited exposure to hard times.

∞

I missed the play in cellular because cellular is outside of my
circle of competence.

I can't be involved in 50 to 75 things. That's a Noah's Ark way of investing—you end up with a zoo that way. I like to put meaningful amounts of money in a few things.

∞

I read annual reports of the company I'm looking at, and I read the annual reports of the competitors—that is the main source of material.

[*On what his favorite companies are like:*] Wonderful castles, surrounded by deep, dangerous moats, where the leader inside is an honest and decent person. Preferably, the castle gets its strength from the genius inside; the moat is permanent and acts as a powerful deterrent to those considering an attack; and inside, the leader makes gold but doesn't keep it all for himself. Roughly translated, we like great companies with dominant positions, whose franchise is hard to duplicate and has tremendous staying power or some permanence to it.

If they try to time their purchases they will do very well for their broker and not very well for themselves.

❧

Interest rates act on financial valuations the way gravity acts on matter. The higher the rate, the greater the downward pull. That's because the rates of return that investors need from any kind of investment are directly tied to the risk-free rate that they can earn from government securities.

All there is to investing is picking good stocks at good times and staying with them as long as they remain good companies.

∞

Talking at business schools, I always say students would be better off if, when they got out of school, they got a ticket with 20 punches on it. And every time they make an investment decision, it uses up a punch. You'll never use up all 20 punches if you save them for the great ideas.

During the 20th Century, the Dow advanced from 66 to 11,497 . . . For investors to merely match that 5.3% market-value gain [today], the Dow—recently below 13,000—would need to close at about 2,000,000 on December 31, 2099 . . . If your adviser talks to you about double-digit returns from equities, explain this math to him—not that it will faze him. Many helpers are apparently direct descendants of the queen in Alice in Wonderland, who said: "Why, sometimes I've believed as many as six impossible things before breakfast."

Problems in a company are like cockroaches in the kitchen.
You will never find just one.

I'd rather have a $10 million business making 15 percent than
a $100 million business making 5 percent.

If you run across one good idea for a business in your lifetime, you're lucky; and fundamentally, Coca-Cola is the best large business in the world. It has got the most powerful brand in the world. It sells for an extremely moderate price. It's universally liked—the per capita consumption goes up almost every year in almost every country. There is no other product like it.

❦

I always picture myself as owning the whole place. And if management is following the same policy that I would follow if I owned the whole place, that's a management I like.

I am a huge bull on this country. We will not have a double-dip recession at all. I see our businesses coming back almost across the board.

⌒∞⌒

Buy a business, don't rent stocks.

If we find a company we like, the level of the market will not really impact our decisions. We will decide company by company. We spend essentially no time thinking about marcroeconomic factors. In other words, if somebody handed us a prediction by the most revered intellectual on the subject, with figures for unemployment or interest rates or whatever it might be for the next two years, we would not pay any attention to it. We simply try to focus on businesses that we think we understand and where we like the price and management. If we see anything that relates to what's going to happen in congress, we don't even read it. We just don't think it's helpful to have a view on these matters.

The best CEOs love operating their companies and don't prefer going to Business Round Table meetings or playing golf at Augusta National.

∽∞∾

I like a business that, when it's not managed at all, still makes lots of money. That's my kind of business.

If you have mediocrity and you have a bunch of friends on the board, it's certainly not the kind of test you put a football team through. If the coach of a football team puts 11 lousy guys out on the field, he loses his job. The board never loses their job because they've got a mediocre CEO. So, you've got none of that self-cleansing type of operation that works with all other jobs.

Diversification is a protection against ignorance. It makes very little sense for those who know what they're doing.

A lot of great fortunes in the world have been made by owning a single wonderful business. If you understand the business, you don't need to own very many of them.

∞

If you have a harem of 40 women, you never get to know any of them very well.

I am quite serious when I say that I do not believe there are, on the whole earth besides, so many intensified bores as in these United States. No man can form an adequate idea of the real meaning of the word, without coming here.

Stocks are simple. All you do is buy shares in a great business for less than the business is intrinsically worth, with managers of the highest integrity and ability. Then you own those shares forever.

Most of our large stock positions are going to be held for many years and the scorecard on our investment decisions will be provided by business results over that period, and not by prices on any given day. Just as it would be foolish to focus unduly on short-term prospects when acquiring an entire company, we think it equally unsound to become mesmerized by the prospective near-term earnings when purchasing small pieces of a company; i.e., marketable common stocks.

Investors making purchases in an overheated market need to recognize that it may often take an extended period for the value of even an outstanding company to catch up with the price they paid.

∽✺∾

I'll make more [acquisition] mistakes in the future—you can bet on that. A line from Bobby Bares' country song explains what too often happens with acquisitions: "I never gone to bed with an ugly women, but I've sure woke up with a few."

Though marginal businesses purchased at cheap prices may be attractive as short-term investments, they are the wrong foundation on which to build a large and enduring enterprise. Selecting a marriage partner clearly requires more demanding criteria than does dating.

The most common cause of low prices is pessimism.

Don't pass up something that's attractive today because you think you will find something more attractive tomorrow.

c∞ɔ

Losing some money is an inevitable part of investing and there is nothing you can do to prevent it.

During the extraordinary financial panic that occurred late in 2008, I never gave a thought to selling my farm or New York real estate, even though a severe recession was clearly brewing. And, if I had owned 100% of a solid business with good long-term prospects, it would have been foolish for me to even consider dumping it. So why would I have sold my stocks that were small participations in wonderful businesses? True, any one of them might eventually disappoint, but as a group they were certain to do well. Could anyone really believe the earth was going to swallow up the incredible productive assets and unlimited human ingenuity existing in America?

The line separating investment and speculation, which is never bright and clear, becomes blurred still further when most market participants have recently enjoyed triumphs. Nothing sedates rationality like large doses of effortless money. After a heady experience of that kind, normally sensible people drift into behavior akin to that of Cinderella at the ball. They know that overstaying the festivities—that is, continuing to speculate in companies that have gigantic valuations relative to the cash they are likely to generate in the future—will eventually bring on pumpkins and mice. But they nevertheless hate to miss a single minute of what is one helluva party. Therefore, the giddy participants all plan to leave just before midnight. There's a problem, though: They are dancing in a room in which the clocks have no hands.

Never risk what you have and need for what you
don't have and don't need.

✦

Our approach is very much profiting from lack of change rather
than from change. With Wrigley chewing gum, it's the lack of
change that appeals to me. I don't think it is going to be hurt by
the Internet. That's the kind of business I like.

We never stretch for yield.

You are neither right nor wrong because the crowd disagrees with you. You are right because your data and reasoning are right.

Unless you can watch your stock holding decline by 50% without becoming panic-stricken, you should not invest in the stock market.

∽∾

Stop trying to predict the direction of the stock market, the economy, interest rates, or elections.

Remember the stock market is manic-depressive.

The greatest investment reward comes to those who by good luck, or good sense, find the occasional company that over the years can grow in sales and profits far more than industry as a whole.

I believe in getting things done through other people.

If you are not happy being in the top one tenth of one percent wealthiest people on earth, being in the top one hundredth of one percent isn't going to do anything for you.

Ted Williams in the science of hitting talks about waiting for the right pitch. And that's what investing is. In batting if you have two strikes you have to swing at the next strike. In investing, you just wait for the next pitch.

∽

I have pledged—to you, the rating agencies, and myself—to always run Berkshire with more than ample cash. We never want to count on the kindness of strangers in order to meet tomorrow's obligations. When forced to choose, I will not trade even a night's sleep for the chance of extra profits.

Risk is a part of God's game, alike for men and nations.

I have no views as to where it [gold] will be, but the one thing
I can tell you is it won't do anything between now and then
except look at you. Whereas, as you know, Coca-Cola will be
making money, and I think Wells Fargo will be making a lot of
money and there will be a lot—and it's a lot—it's a lot better to
have a goose that keeps laying eggs than a goose that just sits
there and eats insurance and storage and a few things like that.

The world will seek low-cost production as long as the quality is there.

⚭

If you are in a poker game and after 20 minutes you don't know who the patsy is, then you're the patsy.

It takes 20 years to build a reputation and five minutes to ruin it. If you think about that, you'll do things differently.

❦

We believe that according the name "investors" to institutions that trade actively is like calling someone who repeatedly engages in one-night stands a "romantic."

Can you really explain to a fish what it's like to walk on land? One day on land is worth a thousand years of talking about it, and one day running a business has exactly the same kind of value.

⁘

Derivatives are financial weapons of mass destruction.

Cash never makes us happy. It's better to have money burning a hole in Berkshire's pocket than resting comfortably in someone else's.

⚯

A very rich person should leave his kids enough to do anything, but not enough to do nothing.

Take me as an example. I happen to have a talent for allocating capital. But my ability to use that talent is completely dependent on the society I was born into. If I'd been born into a tribe of hunters, this talent of mine would be pretty worthless. I can't run very fast. I'm not particularly strong. I'd probably end up as some wild animal's dinner.

∽

The 400 of us pay a lower part of our income in taxes than our receptionists do, or our cleaning ladies, for that matter. If you are the luckiest 1 percent of humanity, you owe it to the rest of humanity to think about the other 99 percent.

If you invested in a very low-cost index fund—where you don't put the money in at one time, but average in over 10 years—you'll do better than 90% of people who start investing at the same time.

⌘

The unconventional, but inescapable, conclusion to be drawn from the past fifty years is that it has been far safer to invest in a diversified collection of American businesses than to invest in securities—Treasures, for example—whose value have been tied to American currency.

Smile when you read a headline that says, "Investors lose as market falls." Edit it in your mind to, "Disinvestors lose as market falls—but investors gain." Though writers often forget this truism, there is a buyer for every seller and what hurts one necessarily helps the other.

∞

We don't get paid for activity, just for being right. As to how long we'll wait, we'll wait indefinitely.

I don't have a problem with guilt about money. The way I see it is that my money represents an enormous number of claim checks on society. It is like I have these little pieces of paper that I can turn into consumption. If I wanted to, I could hire 10,000 people to do nothing but paint my picture every day for the rest of my life. And the GNP would go up. But the utility of the product would be zilch, and I would be keeping those 10,000 people from doing AIDS research, or teaching, or nursing. I don't do that though. I don't use very many of those claim checks. There's nothing material I want very much. And I'm going to give virtually all of those claim checks to charity when my wife and I die.

Over the years, Charlie [Munger] and I have observed
many accounting-based frauds of staggering size. Few of the
perpetrators have been punished; many have not even been
censured. It has been far safer to steal large sums with pen than
small sums with a gun.

～⌘～

Our future rates of gain will fall far short of those achieved in
the past. Berkshire's capital base is now simply too large to allow
us to earn truly outsized returns. If you believe otherwise, you
should consider a career in sales but avoid one in mathematics
(bearing in mind that there are really only three kinds of people
in the world: those who can count and those who can't).

I always knew I was going to be rich. I don't think I ever doubted it for a minute.

∞

Intrinsic value can be defined simply: It is the discounted value of the cash that can be taken out of a business during its remaining life. The calculation of intrinsic value, though, is not so simple. As our definition suggests, intrinsic value is an estimate rather than a precise figure, and it is additionally an estimate that must be changed if interest rates move or forecasts of future cash flows are revised.

We will reject interesting opportunities rather than over-leverage our balance sheet.

❦

Big opportunities come infrequently. When it's raining gold, reach for a bucket, not a thimble.

A pin lies in wait for every bubble. And when the two eventually meet, a new wave of investors learns some very old lessons.

∞

Honesty is a very expensive gift. Don't expect it from cheap people.

A hyperactive stock market is the pickpocket of enterprise.

The most important thing to do if you find yourself in a hole
is to **stop digging.**

None of this means, however, that a business or stock is an intelligent purchase simply because it is unpopular; a contrarian approach is just as foolish as a follow-the-crowd strategy. What's required is thinking rather than polling. Unfortunately, Bertrand Russell's observation about life in general applies with unusual force in the financial world: "Most men would rather die than think. Many do."

If you like spending 6–8 hours per week on investments, do it. If you don't, then dollar-cost average into index funds. This accomplishes diversification across assets and time, two very important things.

Why should I buy real estate when the stock market is so easy?

The one thing I will tell you is the worst investment you can have is cash. Everybody is talking about cash being king and all that sort of thing. Cash is going to become worth less over time. But good businesses are going to become worth more over time.

∞

I think the worst mistake you can make in stocks is to buy or sell based on current headlines.

Charlie [Munger] and I have always considered a "bet" on ever-rising U.S. prosperity to be very close to a sure thing. Indeed, who has ever benefited during the past 237 years by betting against America? If you compare our country's present condition to that existing in 1776, you have to rub your eyes in wonder. And the dynamism embedded in our market economy will continue to work its magic. America's best days lie ahead.

❦

[*On his farm and New York commercial real estate property:*] With my two small investments I thought only of what the properties would produce and cared not at all about their daily valuations. Games are won by players who focus on the playing field—not by those whose eyes are glued to the scoreboard. If you can enjoy Saturdays and Sundays without looking at stock prices, give it a try on weekdays.

Forming macro opinions or listening to the macro or market
predictions of others is a waste of time. Indeed, it is dangerous
because it may blur your vision of the facts that are truly important.
(When I hear TV commentators glibly opine on what the market
will do next, I am reminded of Mickey Mantle's scathing comment:
"You don't know how easy this game is until you get into that
broadcasting booth.")

The market, like the Lord, helps those who help themselves.

If "investors" frenetically bought and sold farmland to each other, neither the yields nor prices of their crops would be increased. The only consequence of such behavior would be decreases in the overall earnings realized by the farm-owning population because of the substantial costs it would occur as it sought advice and switched properties. Nevertheless, both individuals and institutions will constantly be urged to be active by those who profit from giving advice or effecting transactions. The resulting frictional costs can be huge and, for investors in aggregate, devoid of benefit. So ignore the chatter, keep your costs minimal, and invest in stocks as you would in a farm.

We intend to continue our practice of working only with people whom we like and admire. This policy not only maximizes our chances for good results, it also ensures us an extraordinary good time.

∽∞∽

I buy expensive suits. They just look cheap on me.

My money, I should add, is where my mouth is: What I advise here is essentially identical to certain instructions I've laid out in my will. My advice to the trustee could not have been more simple: Put 10% of the cash in short-term government bonds and 90% in a very low-cost S&P 500 index fund (I suggest Vanguard's). I believe the trust's long-term results from this policy will be superior to those attained by most investors—whether pension funds, institutions, or individuals—who employ high-fee managers.

The "when" [*of investing*] is also important. The main danger is that the timid or beginning investor will enter the market at a time of extreme exuberance and then become disillusioned when paper losses occur. (Remember the late Barton Biggs's observation: "A bull market is like sex. It feels best just before it ends.") The antidote to that kind of mistiming is for an investor to accumulate shares over a long period and never sell when the news is bad and stocks are well off their highs. Following those rules, the "know-nothing" investor who both diversifies and keeps costs minimal is virtually certain to get satisfactory results.

The lower prices go, as long as you know the company you're investing in, the better it is for a buyer. Down days always make me feel good.

⌒∞⌒

I learned most of the thoughts in this investment discussion from Ben [Graham]'s book *The Intelligent Investor*, which I bought in 1949. My financial life changed with that purchase. . . . For me, the key points were laid out in what later editions labeled Chapters 8 and 20. (The original 1949 edition numbered its chapters differently.) These points guide my investing decisions today. . . . Of all the investments I ever made, buying Ben's book was the best (except for my purchase of two marriage licenses).

An irresistible footnote: in 1971, pension fund managers invested a record 122% of net funds available in equities—at full prices they couldn't buy enough of them. In 1974, after the bottom had fallen out, they committed a then record low of 21% to stocks.

It's simply to say that managers and investors alike must understand that accounting numbers are the beginning, not the end, of business valuation.

The worst sort of business is one that grows rapidly, requires significant capital to engender the growth, and then earns little or no money. Think airlines. Here a durable competitive advantage has proven elusive ever since the days of the Wright Brothers. Indeed, if a farsighted capitalist had been present at Kitty Hawk, he would have done his successors a huge favor by shooting Orville down.

⌁∞⌁

I've reluctantly discarded the notion of my continuing to manage the portfolio after my death—abandoning my hope to give new meaning to the term "thinking outside the box."

The single most important decision in evaluating a business
is pricing power. If you have the power to raise prices without
losing business to a competitor, you've got a very good business.
And if you have to have a prayer session before raising the price
by a tenth of a cent, then you've got a terrible business.

✑

The key to investing is not assessing how much an industry is
going to effect society, or how much it will grow, but rather
determining the competitive advantage of any given company
and, above all, the durability of that advantage.

The smarter the journalists are, the better off society is. For to a degree, people read the press to inform themselves—and the better the teacher, the better the student body.

∞

Beware of geeks bearing formulas.

If you understood a business perfectly and the future of the business, you would need very little in the way of a margin of safety. So, the more vulnerable the business is, assuming you still want to invest in it, the larger margin of safety you'd need. If you're driving a truck across a bridge that says it holds 10,000 pounds and you've got a 9,800 pound vehicle, if the bridge is 6 inches above the crevice it covers, you may feel okay, but if it's over the Grand Canyon, you may want a little larger margin of safety.

Your premium brand had better be delivering something special, or it's not going to get the business.

⚯

You know, people talk about this being an uncertain time. You know, all time is uncertain. I mean, it was uncertain back in—in 2007, we just didn't know it was uncertain. It was uncertain on September 10th, 2001. It was uncertain on October 18th, 1987, you just didn't know it.

I insist on a lot of time being spent, almost every day, to just sit and think. That is very uncommon in American business. I read and think. So I do more reading and thinking, and make less impulse decisions than most people in business. I do it because I like this kind of life.

∞

No matter how great the talent or efforts, some things just take time. You can't produce a baby in one month by getting nine women pregnant.

I could end the deficit in 5 minutes. You just pass a law that says that anytime there is a deficit of more than 3% of GDP all sitting members of Congress are ineligible for reelection.

∞

Never ask a barber if you need a haircut.

When you combine ignorance and leverage, you get some pretty interesting results.

∞

You know . . . you keep doing the same things and you keep getting the same result over and over again.

A public opinion poll is no substitute for thought.

⁓∞⁓

An irony of inflation-induced financial requirements is that the highly profitable companies—generally the best credits—require relatively little debt capital. But the laggards in profitability never can get enough. Lenders understand this problem much better than they did a decade ago—and are correspondingly less willing to let capital-hungry, low-profitability enterprises leverage themselves to the sky.

The difference between successful people and very successful people is that very successful people say "no" to almost everything.

∞

Intensity is the price of excellence.

A horse that can count to ten is a remarkable horse—not a remarkable mathematician.

Those people who can sit quietly for decades when they own a farm or apartment house too often become frantic when they are exposed to a stream of stock quotations and accompanying commentators delivering an implied message of "Don't just sit there—do something." For these investors, liquidity is transformed from the unqualified benefit it should be to a curse.

Buy into a company because you want to own it,
not because you want the stock to go up.

Love is the greatest advantage a parent can give.

⌗

It's like choosing the 2020 Olympic team by picking the children of all the winners at the 2000 Games.

People will always try to stop you doing the right thing if it is unconventional.

⁕

Do not save what is left after spending, but what is left after saving.

I wouldn't mind going to jail if I had three cellmates who played bridge.

∽◊∾

My successor will need one other particular strength: the ability to fight off the ABCs of business decay, which are arrogance, bureaucracy, and complacency.

[Gold] gets dug out of the ground in Africa, or someplace. Then we melt it down, dig another hole, bury it again, and pay people to stand around guarding it. It has no utility. Anyone watching from Mars would be scratching their head.

⟳

Some material things make my life more enjoyable; many, however, would not. I like having an expensive private plane, but owning a half-dozen homes would be a burden. Too often, a vast collection of possessions ends up possessing its owner. The asset I most value, aside from health, is interesting, diverse, and long-standing friends.

My wealth has come from a combination of living in America, some lucky genes, and compound interest. Both my children and I won what I call the ovarian lottery. (For starters, the odds against my 1930 birth taking place in the U.S. were at least 30 to 1. My being male and white also removed huge obstacles that a majority of Americans then faced.) My luck was accentuated by my living in a market system that sometimes produces distorted results, though overall it serves our country well. I've worked in an economy that rewards someone who saves the lives of others on a battlefield with a medal, rewards a great teacher with thank-you notes from parents, but rewards those who can detect the mispricing of securities with sums reaching into the billions. In short, fate's distribution of long straws is wildly capricious.

It's a mistake paying attention to the day to day fluctuations of a stock—it makes no difference.

If options aren't a form of compensation, what are they? If compensation isn't an expense, what is it? And, if expenses shouldn't go into the calculation of earnings, where in the world should they go?

Managements that say or imply during a public offering that their stock is undervalued are usually being economical with the truth or uneconomical with their existing shareholders' money.

∞

We want our managers to think about what counts, not how it will be counted.

Getting fired can produce a particularly bountiful payday for a CEO. Indeed he can "earn" more in that single day, while cleaning out his desk, than an American worker earns in a lifetime of cleaning toilets. Forget the old maxim about nothing succeeding like success: Today, in the executive suite, the all-too-prevalent rule is that nothing succeeds like failure.

Charlie [Munger] and I love newspapers—we each read five a day.

You can't precisely know what a stock is worth, so leave yourself a margin of safety. Only go into things where you could be wrong to some extent and come out OK.

∞

Borrowed money is the most common way that smart guys go broke.

The happiest people do not necessarily have the best things.
They simply appreciate the things they have.

∽∞∾

There comes a time when you ought to start doing what you
want. Take a job that you love. You will jump out of bed in the
morning. I think you are out of your mind if you keep taking
jobs that you don't like because you think it will look good on
your resume. Isn't that a little like saving up sex for your old age?

In order not to make too many stupid things, it's enough to make a few very important things.

The great personal fortunes in this country weren't built on a portfolio of 50 companies. They were built by someone who identified one wonderful business.

Lethargy bordering on sloth should remain the cornerstone of investment style.

∞

Life is like a snowball. The important thing is finding wet snow and a really long hill.

Never test the depth of the river with both feet.

The stock doesn't know you own it. You have feelings about it, but it has no feelings about you. The stock doesn't know what you paid. People shouldn't get emotionally involved with their stocks.

Most institutional investors in the early 1970s, on the other hand, regarded business value as of only minor relevance when they were deciding prices at which they would buy or sell. This now seems hard to believe. However, these institutions were then under the spell of academics at prestigious business schools who were preaching a newly-fashioned theory: the stock market was totally efficient, and therefore calculations of business value—and even thought, itself—were of no more importance in investment activities. (We are enormously indebted to these academics: what could be more advantageous in an intellectual contest—whether it be bridge, chess, or stock selection—than to have opponents who have been taught that thinking is a waste of energy?)

I bought a company in the mid-'90s called Dexter Shoe and paid $400 million for it. And I gave about $400 million worth of Berkshire stock, which is probably now worth $400 billion. But I've made lots of dumb decisions. That's part of the game.

❦

You have no ability, if you're a financial institution and you're threatened with criminal prosecution, you have no ability to negotiate.

The rich are always going to say that, you know, just give us more money and we'll go out and spend more and then it will trickle down to the rest of you. But that has not worked the last 10 years, and I hope the American public is catching on.

∞

Diversification may preserve wealth, but concentration builds wealth.

The best business returns are usually achieved by companies that are doing something quite similar today to what they were doing five or ten years ago.

Money to some extent sometimes lets you be in more interesting environments. But it can't change how many people love you or how healthy you are.

I've seen more people fail because of liquor and leverage—
leverage being borrowed money. You really don't need
leverage in the world much. If you're smart, you're going to
make a lot of money without borrowing.

Your goal as an investor should simply be to purchase, at a rational price, a part interest in an easily-understandable business whose earnings are virtually certain to be materially higher five, ten and twenty years from now. Over time, you will find only a few companies that meet these standards—so when you see one that qualifies, you should buy a meaningful amount of stock. You must also resist the temptation to stray from your guidelines: If you aren't willing to own a stock for ten years, don't even think about owning it for ten minutes. Put together a portfolio of companies whose aggregate earnings march upward over the years, and so also will the portfolio's market value.